Benjamin Britten

A Boy was Born

Choral Variations for Men's, Women's and Boys' Voices
(Organ Accompaniment ad libitum)

Revised edition and organ accompaniment 1958

CHESTER MUSIC

CONTENTS

NOTES ON PERFORMANCE

1. Throughout the work, a dot above or below a note signifies a separation of that note from the one immediately following it. True staccato is indicated by a dash (▾).

2. Breathing marks are indicated by a tick (√). A comma (,) signifies a break in the time, which the former does not.

3. The Latin pronunciation of 'Jesu'—'Yaysoo'—is to be used throughout the work.

ACKNOWLEDGEMENTS

The various poems from *Ancient English Christmas Carols*, collected and arranged by Edith Rickert, are reprinted by her kind permission and that of the publishers, Messrs. Chatto & Windus.

The words of *A Boy was Born* and of *Welcome be Thou* are reprinted by permission from the *Oxford Book of Carols*.

THEME
'A BOY WAS BORN' *

A BOY WAS BORN in Bethlehem;
Rejoice for that, Jerusalem!
Alleluya.

He let himself a servant be,
That all mankind he might set free:
Alleluya.

Then praise the Word of God who came
To dwell within a human frame:
Alleluya.

VARIATION I
'LULLAY, JESU' †

Mine own dear mother, sing lullay!
Lullay, Jesu, lullay, lullay!
Mine own dear mother, sing lullay!

So blessed a sight it was to see,
How Mary rocked her Son so free;
So fair she rocked and sang 'by-by.'

'Therefore, mother, weep I nought,
But for the woe that shall be wrought
To me, ere I mankind have bought.

'Mine own dear Son, why weepest Thou thus?
Is not Thy father King of bliss?
Have I not done that in me is?
Your grievance, tell me what it is.'

'Ah, dear mother! yet shall a spear
My heart in sunder all to-tear;
No wonder though I careful were.

'Now, dear mother, sing lullay,
    And put away all heaviness;
Into this world I took the way,
    Again to (heaven) I shall me dress,
Where joy is without end ay,
    Mine own dear mother, sing lullay!'
    Lullay, Jesu, lullay, lullay!
    Mine own dear mother, sing lullay!

* German (sixteenth century)—trans. N.S.T.
(Oxford Book of Carols)

† Anon. (before 1536)
(Ancient English Christmas Carols)

VARIATION II
HEROD *

Noel!

Herod that was both wild and wode,
Full much he shed of Christian blood,
To slay the Child so meek of mood,
That Mary bare, that clean may [1].

Herod slew with pride and sin
Thousands of two year and within;
The body of Christ he thought to win
And to destroy the Christian fay [2].

Mary with Jesu forth yfraught [3],
As the angel her taught,
To flee the land till it were sought,
To Egypt she took her way.

Now Jesus that didst die for us on the Rood,
And didst christen innocents in their blood,
By the prayer of Thy mother good,
Bring us to bliss that lasteth ay.

VARIATION III
'JESU, AS THOU ART OUR SAVIOUR' *

Jesu, Jesu, Jesu, Jesu,
Save us all through Thy virtue.

Jesu, as Thou art our Saviour
That Thou save us fro dolour!
Jesu is mine paramour.
    Blessed be Thy name, Jesu.

Jesu was born of a may,
Upon Christëmas Day,
She was may beforn and ay,
    Blessed be Thy name, Jesu.

VARIATION IV
THE THREE KINGS *

There came three kings fro Galilee
Into Bethlehem, that fair city,
To seek Him that should ever be
              by right–a,
Lord and king and knight–a.

They took their leave, both old and ying,
Of Herod, that moody king;
They went forth with their offering
              by light–a,
By the star that shone so bright–a.

Till they came into the place
Where Jesus and His mother was,
Offered they up with great solace
              in fere–a [4]
Gold, incense, and myrrh–a.

Forth then went these kingës three,
Till they came home to their country;
Glad and blithe they were all three
Of the sight that they had see
              bydene–a [5].

*Anon. (fifteenth century)
(Ancient English Christmas Carols)

[1] maid
[2] faith
[3] laden
[4] together
[5] together

VARIATION V
'IN THE BLEAK MID-WINTER'

* In the bleak mid-winter
  Frosty wind made moan,
Earth stood hard as iron,
  Water like a stone;
Snow had fallen, snow on snow,
  Snow on snow,
In the bleak mid-winter
  Long ago.

† *Lully, lulley, lully, lulley,*
  The falcon hath borne my make¹ away.

He bare him up, he bare him down,
He bare him into an orchard brown.

In that orchard there was an hall
That was hangëd with purple and pall.

And in that hall there was a bed,
It was hangëd with gold so red.

In that bed there lieth a knight,
His woundës bleeding, day and night.

By that bedside kneeleth a may,
And she weepeth both night and day.

And by that bedside there standeth a stone,
Corpus Christi written thereon.

VARIATION VI (FINALE)
NOEL!

Noel! Wassail!

† *Good day, good day,*
  My Lord Sir Christëmas, good day!

Good day, Sir Christëmas our King,
For every man, both old and ying,
Is glad of your coming.
  Good day.

Godës Son so much of might
From heaven to earth down is light
And born is of a maid so bright.
  Good day.

Noel! Our King!
Hosanna!
This night a Child is born

* Christina G. Rossetti
† Anon. (fifteenth century)
(Ancient English Christmas Carols)

¹ mate

*Get ivy and hull[1], woman, deck up thine house,
    And take this same brawn for to seethe and to souse;
    Provide us good cheer, for thou knowest the old guise,
    Old customs that good be, let no man despise.
    At Christmas be merry and thank God of all,
    And feast thy poor neighbours, the great and the small.
    Yea, all the year long have an eye to the poor,
    And God shall send luck to keep open thy door.
    Good fruit and good plenty do well in thy loft,
    Then lay for an orchard and cherish it oft.
    The profit is mickle, the pleasure is much;
    At pleasure with profit few wise men will grutch.
    For plants and for stocks lay aforehand to cast,
    But set or remove them, while Twelve-tide do last.

† Welcome be Thou, heaven-king,
    Welcome born in one morning,
    Welcome for whom we shall sing
        Welcome Yule.

Welcome be ye that are here,
Welcome all, and make good cheer,
Welcome all another year!
    Welcome Yule.

‡ Glory to God on high, and jolly mirth
    'Twixt man and man, and peace on earth!

Wassail, Wassail! ...
Lully, lulley, lully, lulley, ...

Noel! Noel! ...
Herod that was so wild and wode.

Mine own dear mother ...
Jesu, Jesu! ...

This night a Child is born ;
    This night a Son is given;
    This Son, this Child
    Hath reconciled
Poor man that was forlorn,
    And the angry God of heaven.
        Hosanna, sing Hosanna!

Now, now that joyful day,
    That blessed hour is come,
    That was foretold
    In days of old,
Wherein all nations may
    Bless, bless the virgin's womb.
        Hosanna, sing Hosanna!

Let heaven triumph above,
    Let earth rejoice below;
    Let heaven and earth
    Be filled with mirth,
For peace and lasting love
    Atones your God and you.
        Hosanna, sing Hosanna!

[1] holly

* Thomas Tusser (1558)
(Ancient English Christmas Carols)

† Anon. (fifteenth century)
(Oxford Book of Carols)

‡ Francis Quarles (1592–1644)
(Ancient English Christmas Carols)

To my Father

A Boy was Born

BENJAMIN BRITTEN
Op.3
[The organ part edited
by Ralph Downes]

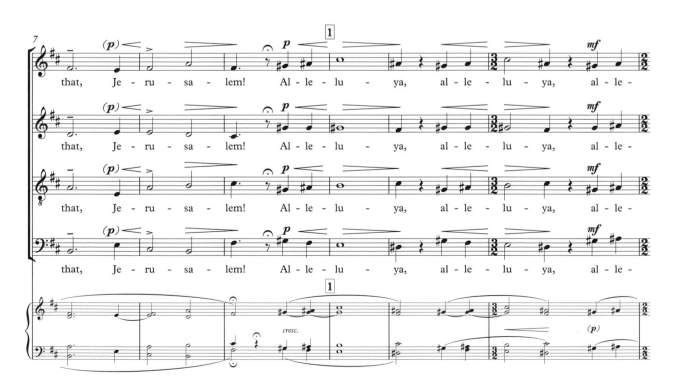

Lullay, Jesu

†Pronounced *Yay-soo*

'Have I not done that

thus?____ Is not Thy fa - - ther King of bliss?____

thus?____ Is not Thy fa - - ther King of bliss?____ Have I not done that

Je - - - su.____ Je - - su.____

Je - - - su.____ Je - - su.____

- lay, lul - lay, lul - lay, lul - lay, lul - lay, lul-

lul - lay, lul - lay, lul - lay, lul - lay, lul - lay,

cresc.

sim.

(without Ped.)

p

54

Herod

*The passages in brackets here and at 21 & 27 to be played when necessary.

28

Jesu, as Thou art our Saviour

†Pronounced *Yay-soo*

The Three Kings

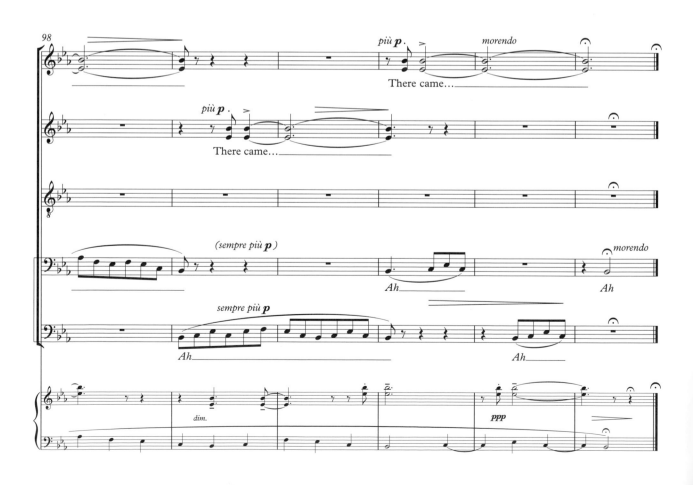

In the Bleak Mid-Winter

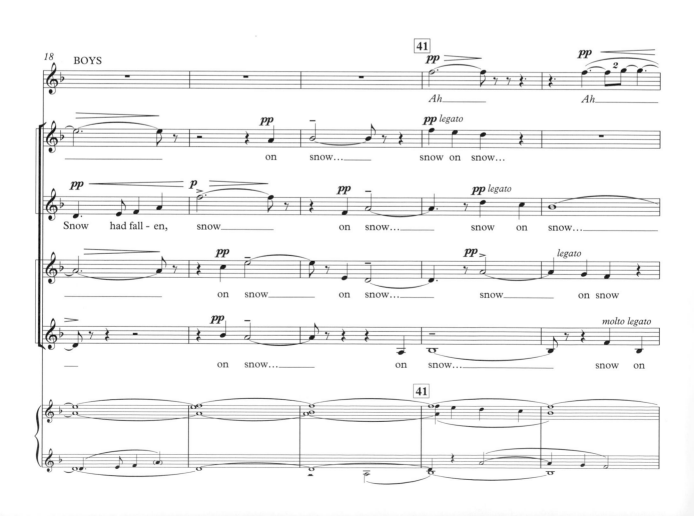

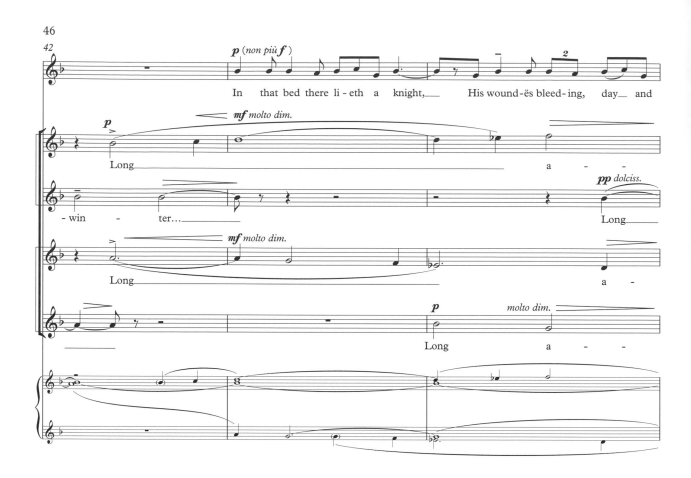

Noel!

56

62

Ped. (Sw. coupled)

Nov. 1932 – May 1933
Revised Oct. 1955